W9-CMO-371

Swimming

Marshall Cavendish
Benchmark
New York

This edition first published in 2010 in North America by Marshall Cavendish Benchmark

Marshall Cavendish Benchmark
99 White Plains Road
Tarrytown, NY 10591
www.marshallcavendish.us

Published in 2009 by Evans Publishing Ltd, 2A Portman Mansions, Chiltern St, London W1U 6NR

Editor: Nicola Edwards
Designer: D.R. Ink
All photgraphs by Wishlist Images except for page 6 © Liu Jin/AFP/Getty Images; page 8 © Simon Bruty /Sports Illustrated/Getty Images; page 11 © Ryan McVay/Getty Images; page 12 © Marcus Brandt/AFP/Getty Images; page 13 © Mik Hewitt/Getty Images; page 14 © Ezra Shaw/Getty Images; page 22 © Arpad Kuruc/Getty Images; page 23 © Cameron Spencer/Getty Images; page 25 © Rich Clarkson/Sports Illustrated/Getty Images; page 26 © Bob Thomas/Getty Images; page 27 © Francois-Xavier Marit/AFP/Getty Images

Library of Congress Cataloging-in-Publication Data

Gifford, Clive.
 Swimming/by Clive Gifford.
    p. cm. — (Tell me about sports)
Includes index.
 Summary: "An introduction to swimming, including techniques, rules, and the training regimen of professional athletes in the sport"—Provided by publisher.
 ISBN 978-0-7614-4462-6
1. Swimming—Juvenile literature. I. Title.
GV837.6. G54 2009b
797.2'1—dc22
                          2008049023

Marshall Cavendish Editor: Megan Comerford

Printed in China.
135642

Contents

Swimming

▲

Competitors in a 100 m breaststroke race at the 2008 Paralympic Games power through the water.

Swimming is an important skill for everyone to learn. It can be lots of fun at a beach or at your local pool. Knowing how to swim can also save your life. You don't have to take part in competitions to enjoy swimming, but testing yourself against other swimmers in races can be very exciting. You will need to be fit and fast to be a winner!

There are both short-distance races, such as the 50 meter (m), and long-distance races in which competitors swim several miles. Swimmers power through the water using different strokes. There are four main strokes in swimming: the front crawl, backstroke, breaststroke, and butterfly.

You don't need a lot of equipment to take part in swimming races. All you need is a comfortable swimsuit that fits you well. If you have long hair, you can tuck it onto a bathing cap. It's a good idea to wear a tracksuit to keep you warm before and after swimming.

Another useful item is a good pair of goggles. These help you see clearly underwater. Always put the goggles over your eyes first and then pull the strap over your head.

▼ Having swimming races with friends can be a lot of fun. These young swimmers wear shirts to keep warm before a race.

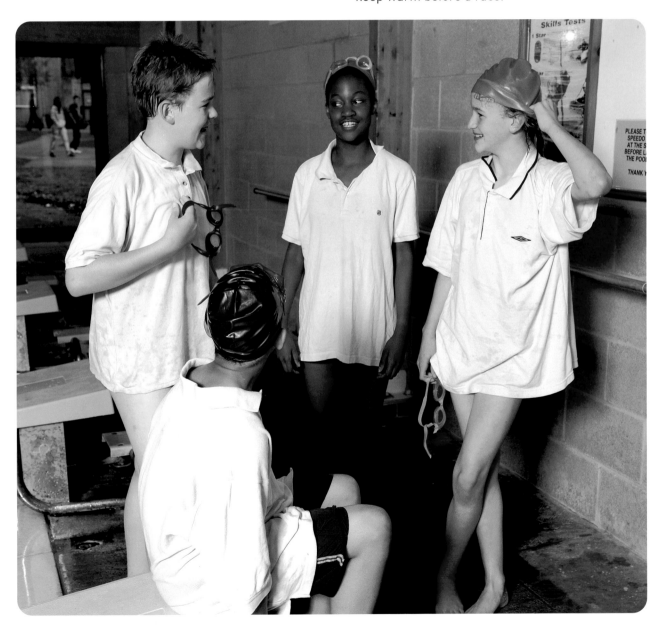

Finishing First

A swimming race ends when all swimmers have swum the full distance and have touched the pool wall in front of them. Every swimmer aims to touch the wall first to win the race.

For most swimmers, the last part of the race is the hardest. Your body tires and it can be a struggle to keep on swimming smoothly. It is in this last part of the race that the strongest swimmers often move to the front.

▼ Great Britain's Rebecca Adlington wins the 400 m freestyle at the 2008 Olympics. She beat Katie Hoff of the United States by just 0.07 of a second!

Many races are lost or won on a swimmer's final surge to the end of the pool. If you stretch out to reach the end of the pool too early, you may lose speed. If you wait too long, someone may touch the wall before you.

In big competitions, close finishes happen all the time. Special electronic touch pads are fitted to the pool walls. These are linked to a computer that works out the swimmers' times to hundredths or thousandths of a second. A giant screen displays these times after a race is over.

Do not get discouraged if you don't do well in a swimming race. Learn from any mistakes you made and work hard to swim faster next time.

Close Finishes

Americans Nancy Hogshead and Carrie Steinseifer could not be separated at the 1984 Olympics. Their 100 m race was the first official **tie** in Olympic history.

At the 2004 Olympics, Gary Hall Jr. of the United States beat Duje Draganja of Croatia in the 50 m freestyle by 0.01 second! At the 2000 Olympics, Hall and his teammate Anthony Ervin tied for the event and both won a gold medal.

▼ There are T-shaped markings on the pool floor. They let swimmers know that they are five meters away from the pool wall.

▼ A young swimmer touches the pool wall before his rivals to win the race.

The Pool

Some swimming races take place in the sea or in a lake. These are known as open-water races. Most races, though, happen in a swimming pool.

Swimming pools vary in length. Short-course swimming events are held in a 25 m pool. Long-course swimming takes place in a 50 m pool. Swimming races at the Olympics are always in a 50 m pool.

▼ Buoys mark the lines in this competition swimming pool. It may seem quiet now, but it will be packed with fans for swim meets.

▲ Many races are more than one length of the pool. Swimmers make special racing turns, somersaulting and pushing off the pool wall to begin their next length.

At the Olympics

Swimming at the first modern Olympics in 1896 was in the open sea. One of the races was only for sailors from Greece.

The 1900 Olympics included a swimming obstacle race in the River Seine!

Open-water swimming returned to the Olympics in 2008 with 10 km races for both men and women.

A competition swimming pool has certain special features. Just like a running track, the pool is divided into eight lanes. The lanes are marked out on the pool floor and also by a string of floats on the top of the water. Swimmers must not leave their lane or they will be **disqualified**.

Most pools have a giant clock on the wall. They also have a line of flags that hang above both ends of the pool. These flags are five meters from each end of the pool. They help backstroke swimmers judge how far they are from the pool wall.

Swimming Stars

Champion swimmers like Michael Phelps and Ian Thorpe are big sports stars. They also train very hard. Each year, top swimmers spend thousands of hours training in the pool and working with their coaches. Many swim over 50,000 meters (30 miles) every week.

▼ U.S. swimmer Dara Torres has some physiotherapy on her leg before a race. Top swimmers need to be in perfect condition to compete well.

Australian star swimmer Leisel Jones has ten pool sessions every week. She also works out in the gym twice a week and has two sessions on an exercise bike. Her training day begins when she gets up at 5:30 a.m.!

Swimmers spend a lot of time stretching their muscles before training or racing. Stretching helps their bodies perform well and stops injuries. Swimmers also eat very healthily. They get advice on their diet from experts.

Most swimmers have to swim in more than one race during a competition. The first races are called **heats**, and only the fastest swimmers from these heats qualify for the next round. As the swimmers take their places for the final race, the pressure is on. Top swimmers want to make all their training count.

▲ Michael Phelps (*right*) roars his approval as his team-mate in the 4 x 100 m relay performs well. Phelps won a record eight gold medals at the 2008 Olympics.

Diving In

The backstroke and races for very young swimmers start in the water. Most races, though, start with the swimmers standing by the side of the pool on boxes called **starting blocks**.

An official called a starter controls the beginning of a race. On the starter's order, you climb onto your block. Your toes curl around the front of the block and you bend over, ready to spring.

▼ American swimmer Cullen Jones begins his dive in the 2007 World Championship 50 m freestyle final. His arms will stretch forward and punch through the water.

▲ Swimmers are coiled up like springs on their blocks. They are ready to make fast, shallow dives into the water.

▲ Swimmers lift their hips and lower their heads when they dive. They aim for their hands to punch a hole through the water. The rest of their body follows.

The starting signal can be a loud whistle blast or a bang from a starter's gun. When you hear the signal, you dive off the block into the water. You should try to **glide** along under the water as smoothly as possible.

Leaving your block early is called a **false start**. At big competitions, a swimmer who makes a false start is disqualified. If there has been a false start, a rope drops into the water ahead of the other swimmers to let them know.

▼ When gliding under the water, try to keep your arms and legs together. You want to be as narrow as possible. This helps you slice through the water.

Freestyle

Freestyle means you can swim any type of stroke you like in a race. In fact, everyone chooses the front crawl in these races because it is the fastest stroke.

To swim the front crawl well, you need to keep your head in the water. Make your body as flat as possible with your legs stretched out behind you.

Your legs kick quickly while your arms provide most of the power. One hand, with fingers together, enters the water ahead of you. It then presses back on the water.

▼ These swimmers do not splash a lot as they swim. This is because their feet remain under the water and their hands enter the water cleanly. Big splashes mean wasted power.

Front Crawl Facts

American Johnny Weissmuller used the front crawl when he became the first person to swim 100 m in less than a minute. He won five Olympic medals and later became famous as Tarzan in the movies.

South African Natalie Du Toit lost her left leg at the knee after a motor accident in 2001. She swims the front crawl without an artificial leg. In 2008, she managed to qualify to swim the 10 km race at the Olympics.

◀ Your legs kick up and down under the water. Stretch your feet and point your toes as you kick.

Your arm travels back underwater. It passes your waist, comes out of the water elbow first, then travels low through the air to begin its next stroke in front of your head. When one arm is entering the water, the other is pushing back.

The front crawl takes plenty of energy. Your legs kick all the time. Both arms work to move you forward. It's important to learn to pace yourself. Don't swim too fast at the start or you will run out of energy before the end of the race.

▶ Instead of lifting your head straight up to breathe, turn your head to one side. Part of your face stays in the water all the time.

Breaststroke

Breaststroke is thought to be the oldest of the main swimming strokes. You can swim breaststroke with your head up out of the water. But to go faster, you need to get your head under! This is how swimmers in races do the stroke.

When swimming the breaststroke, you want to make your body lie as flat as possible in the water. Your hips

▼ As your hands come under your chin, your head comes out of the water. Take a breath before you go back under the water. From this position, you stretch your arms in front of you and sweep them out to the sides.

stay near the surface and your arms and legs stay in the water all the time. Move your arms out in front of you so that your body is stretched long. Then, sweep both hands out and around ending with your hands below your chin. Your arms make a heart-shaped pattern.

Look at the sequence of photos at the bottom of this page. As your arms move, your feet kick in a sort of circle as well. Both feet move at the same time.

In races, the breaststroke is the slowest of the strokes, but is still powerful if swum well. In a breaststroke race, both hands have to touch the pool wall at the same time when making a turn or finishing the race.

▼ Your knees bend, bringing your feet up toward your rear end.

▼ Your feet point out toward either side.

▼ Your legs go straight again with your knees just touching.

Backstroke

The backstroke, or back crawl, is the only one of the four main strokes in which your face isn't in the water. It is also the only one where you start a race already in the water.

At a major race, the pool wall has special bars for swimmers to hold. You pull yourself up into a tuck position with your chin near your chest. If there are no bars, you grip the edge of the pool.

On the starter's whistle or pistol, you fling your arms back and push off really hard with both feet. You push your stomach up to arch your back. Your hands and arms are the first things to enter the water. It's like a backward dive.

▼ Swimmers start a backstroke race. Although their bodies rise out of the water on the start, their feet must remain in the water.

The backstroke movement is similar to the front crawl. Your legs kick up and down from the hips. One arms travels through the air while the other one sweeps down, pulling through the water.

A common mistake is to let your rear end drop low. Try to keep your body nice and flat and most of your head under the water.

▼ This swimmer's right arm travels high through the air. His head faces the ceiling and stays as straight as possible.

▲ See how narrow the swimmer looks. This is called being streamlined. A streamlined shape allows you to cut through the water faster.

Backstroke Facts

Hungary's Krisztina Egerszegi became the youngest Olympic swimming champion in 1988. At age 14 she won the 200 m backstroke.

In 2007, Aaron Piersol of the United States became the first person to swim the 100 m backstroke in less than 53 seconds.

Butterfly

▲ France's Malia Metella swims the butterfly during the 2006 European Swimming Championships. Her body stays symmetrical throughout her stroke.

Invented in the 1950s, the butterfly is the newest stroke in swimming races. It is also the most spectacular. Swimmers surge forward with their arms coming out of the water.

You need to be fit and a good swimmer to swim the butterfly. It is probably the last of the main strokes you will learn. It is best to practice it in short distances.

Both arms work together. Your elbows leave the water first and then your arms pass low over the surface. Your hands stay about shoulder-width apart as they enter the water ahead of you. As your arms pull through the water, you can raise your head above the surface to take a breath.

While your arms are moving, your legs are moving, too. Both legs perform the same movement at the same time. They stay close together and travel up and down together. This is called the dolphin kick.

▲ See how the head rises just enough for you to take a breath.

▲ Your legs are moving up and down together with your feet stretched.

▲ Once in the water, your arms sweep outward and then inward.

▼ Michael Phelps cuts through the water as his head rises to take a breath. Top swimmers often only breathe every second stroke.

Relays and Medleys

Relay races are for teams of four swimmers. At the Olympics, there are two relay events: the 4 x 100 m and the 4 x 200 m. All swimmers swim the same distance, either 100 m or 200 m.

One swimmer starts his or her distance. Meanwhile, the next swimmer gets on the starting block and waits until their teammate touches the pool wall before diving in. Relay competitors swim the front crawl. Some teams put their strongest swimmer on the last leg of the relay to make up any lost time.

▼ Swimmers in a relay race get ready to dive in as their teammates finish up.

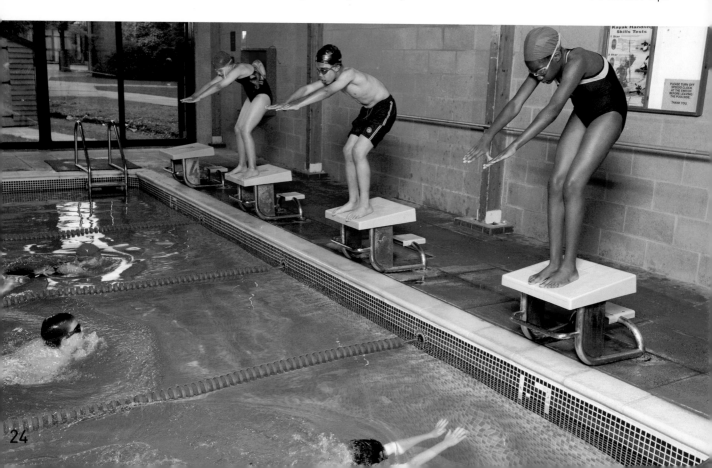

Relays and Records

U.S. swimmer Gertrude Ederle won a gold medal in the 4 x 100 m relay at the 1924 Olympics. In 1926 she became the first woman to swim the English Channel.

Stephanie Rice of Australia broke the 400 m Individual Medley world record in 2008. Three days later, she broke the 200 m Individual Medley world record, as well.

In medley races swimmers use all four of the main strokes. In **medley relays**, four-person teams compete. Each swimmer swims one of the strokes. **Individual medleys** are tough races. You have to swim each of the four strokes yourself. You start with the butterfly, then do the backstroke and the breaststroke. You finish with the front crawl.

▲ Relay and medley teammates encourage each other and train together.

▶
The **changeover** in a relay race can be hard to follow. Officials watch each lane, checking to see that the changeover between swimmers is correct.

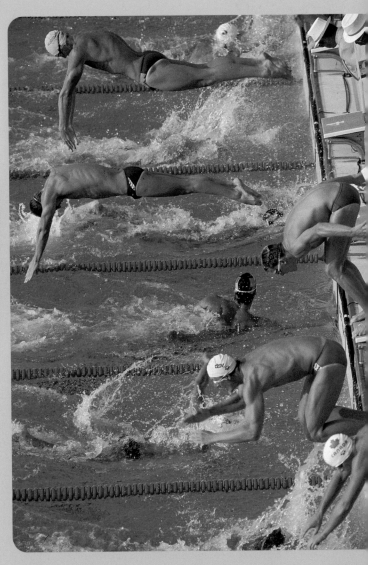

The World of Swimming

The greatest swimming competition is at the Olympic Games. Every four years, thousands of fans fill an Olympic aquatic center and watch the wide range of swimming races. Millions more watch the events at home on TV.

▼At the 2004 Olympics, the men's 200 m freestyle final was an exciting race. Australia's Ian Thorpe (lane 5) beat Pieter van den Hoogenband of The Netherlands (lane 4) and Michael Phelps of the United States (lane 3).

Competition is tough at the Olympics. The two leading countries in swimming are Australia and the United States. Other nations, such as The Netherlands, Russia, Germany, and the United Kingdom, also have strong teams. To get onto a country's Olympic team, swimmers have to win races called trials or do well in their national swimming championship.

The World Aquatic Championships is a major event. It is held every two years. It was held in 2009 in Rome, Italy. Diving and water polo sports are included in addition to the swimming events.

During the 2007 championships in Australia, fifteen world records were broken, five by American swimmer Michael Phelps!

A world championship for short-course swimming in a 25 m pool is also held every two years. The last was in Manchester, England, and the 2010 competition will be held in Dubai.

Great Champions

In 1972, American Mark Spitz won an incredible seven Olympic gold medals in swimming.

At the 2008 Olympics, Michael Phelps broke Spitz's amazing record. He won eight gold medals.

American Natalie Coughlan has won more World Championship swimming medals than any other woman. She has six gold, six silver, and four bronze medals.

▼ Australia's Liesel Jones powers down her lane during a heat for the 2008 Olympics 200 m breaststroke. Jones won a silver medal in this event to go with her career total of three Olympic and seven World Championship gold medals.

Where Next?

These websites and books will help you to find out more about swimming.

Websites

http://www.fina.org

This is the website of FINA, The International Swimming Federation, the organization that runs world swimming. You can read all about the top swimmers and competitions.

http://www.totalimmersion.net/

This website offers a monthly swimming magazine and great video lessons that are free to download.

http://www.usaswimming.org/

There is information about top American swimmers as well as swimming and training tips at this website.

Books

Kehm, Greg. *Olympic Swimming and Diving* (Great Moments in Olympic History).
   New York: Rosen, 2007.

Miller, Amanda. *Let's Talk Swimming*. New York: Children's Press, 2008.

Swimming Words

changeover The part during a relay race when one swimmer finishes his or her leg and the next swimmer begins.

disqualified Removed from a swimming race for breaking a rule.

false start An error made by a swimmer who enters the pool or starts a race before the starter has given the signal.

glide Move smoothly through the water without moving your arms and legs.

heat An early race in an event. The fastest swimmers in a heat enter the semifinals or final.

individual medley A race in which you swim an equal distance using all four swimming strokes.

medley relay A relay race where each swimmer swims a different stroke.

starting blocks Raised platforms for swimmers to stand on at the start of many races.

relay A race for teams of swimmers, with four people in each team. When one swimmer finishes his or her lap, the next swimmer starts the next leg.

tie When two swimmers finish a race at exactly the same time.

Index

Numbers in **bold** refer to pictures.